RELIGION & THE PARANORMAL BK 1

MR. JERRY SAENZ

iUniverse, Inc.
New York   Bloomington

Religion & The Paranormal Bk 1

iUniverse books may be ordered through booksellers or by contacting:

*iUniverse
1663 Liberty Drive
Bloomington, IN 47403
www.iuniverse.com
1-800-Authors (1-800-288-4677)*

*Because of the dynamic nature of the Internet, any Web addresses or
links contained in this book may have changed since publication and
may no longer be valid. The views expressed in this work are solely those
of the author and do not necessarily reflect the views of the publisher,
and the publisher hereby disclaims any responsibility for them.*

*ISBN: 978-1-4401-2010-7 (sc)
ISBN: 978-1-4401-2011-4 (ebook)*

Library of Congress Control Number: 2009925374

Printed in the United States of America

iUniverse rev. date: 3/11/2009

Contents

Introduction

Before I begin, let me introduce myself, my name is Jerry and I'm a psychic, I started receiving messages at the age of thirty three years old. I have been connected to the spirit world prior since my early years but did not start receiving information from the angels until the age of thirty three. I want you the reader to understand that the angel spirits communicate at high rates of speed. It is difficult for them to slow down to the point where they can communicate at a rate considered normal.

This presents a challenge when trying to write down the information as quickly as it comes in. This is also the reason that I jump into different subjects regarding the paranormal and my own experiences.

Therefore I apologize for the fragmented manner in which some of the material is introduced.

The information presented here is based on what I wanted to know and wanted to ask, which I believed would interest other individuals as well, regarding energy started to form, and three elderly people appeared. There were two elderly women and one elderly man, and all three were sitting down in chairs and talking to me in Spanish.

When I was done talking to them, I immediately went to look for mother to ask her who these people were. She was startled when I told her and ran to the bedroom, where were these people. When we went to the room no one was there. She then called me a liar and said that I should not make up stories. I argued with her that what happened was true, but she didn't believe me or what I had seen.

I sometimes saw events; that had not yet occurred, I thought they had. I also saw a lot of imprint energy, which I did not understand at the time, because I was unaware of such phenomena as a child. I eventually learned that it was residual energy left behind, that at times repeats itself under certain conditions.

Throughout my childhood these types of incidents occurred, and as usual, I was deemed a liar. But I was seven years old, and like most people in 1961, I knew nothing about being psychic. I wish I had known someone who could have mentored me at that time.

Unfortunately, due to religious upbringing and ignorance in the Hispanic culture, this type of gift was viewed in a negative fashion. I eventually learned to keep quiet and not mention any more phenomena.

Different Thoughts and Ideas Growing Up

When I was in the fifth grade, I was already trying to create a laser light from a bright red light that belonged to a Phillips phonograph, and through the use of magnifying glasses I tried to create a fine beam of light, then I was in the seventh grade I was trying to figure out how to transfer television signals on to cassette tapes, in other words, the first video recorders. But I was just a kid with six siblings and a poor family, so I lacked resources and money.

I had trouble communicating with others because my ideas were ahead of their time, and everyone thought I was crazy.

Over forty years if you told some one that you were going to invent a disc that would play music through a laser light, they thought you were nuts.

There weren't even computers that could do such a thing. In 1967, any type of computer was binary, took up the space of a whole building and could do only simple functions.

My two brothers could never comprehend my thoughts or what I was trying to conceive. It was hard for me to have intelligent conversations growing up in the Barrios.

Most of the Hispanics were into cars, beer, booze, women, and sports. I wanted to talk about different subject matters, such as science-fiction, science, biology, and other intelligent subjects. So I had to limit my conversations or subjects to a lower understanding due to my social environment.

Experiencing the Paranormal at a Young Age

From the time that I was a thirteen, I had numerous nighttime experiences of alien abduction. They communicated with me through telepathy. They appeared in human form and told me that they were from a very distant planet in our galaxy.

They were friendly towards me and frequently picked me up throughout my teen years. They picked me up in some type of shuttle that was beige in color and their uniforms were beige in color as well and the shuttle looked something like a large van that flew but it did not have wheels. This type of activity continued until I was about nineteen years of age then, a small metal type chip fell out of my nasal cavity, the abductions stopped.

In addition to those experiences, I also saw creatures and beings from other dimensions. They came out at night: black figures in human shape but without faces and fingers, appearing and disappearing

while. It turns out to be the new war that George W. Bush is about to start.

I saw 9/11 about a week before it happened, I told my wife about it, but I asked who would believe me. If I told what I saw, people would think I was some nut and arrest me.

I also saw the flooding of New Orleans and other states along the Gulf of Mexico.

In my sleep at night I started seeing murders take place. I'm able to see the murders through the eyes of the murderer, and the eyes of the victim. I also see street names and locations. But I'm afraid to contact the police, for two following reasons:

First, I'm Hispanic and I fear that I will be accused of the crime. This has happened to many psychics who came forward and knew a great deal about the crime. They became victims of police officers looking for someone to pin the crime on.

Second whose will believe me? I have doubts about my powers, so what if I'm wrong or can't prove what I saw.

I have a good job as construction inspector, I could lose my job is they think that I'm some type of nut.

Astral Projection and Dreams

Other experiences I started having were astral projection episodes, this also started at the age of thirty three. During these episodes, I go to other dimensions of earth. There are seventy- two total dimensions of Earth, and in each dimension your life is different.

I also learned that there are differences in dreams, and interpretations. Some dreams are a compilation of events that happened throughout the day. Other dreams are messages about changes you need to make in your life. Some dreams are not dreams they are visions showing events that will take place in the future.

Other dream like states, are experiences of astral projection which can actually take to you to certain locations where events are taking place. Another astral projection experience lets you visit your relatives on the other side. A third astral projection experience lets you visit alternate dimensions, with alternate lives.

I've experienced numerous types of the above. Some experiences were beautiful. When you visit the other side, you can see relatives, that you miss and actually spend time with them and other family members. In these experiences, they can actually give you messages.

Then there are dreams where family members on the other side are communicating with you through images in the dream. You must interpret the symbols, to understand the message.

The Angels told me that people on the other side don't often appear to family members on this side, because most people would die of fright if they saw deceased loved one appear. Also some family members don't believe that there is life after death.

The Angels said that if you believe and accept that your relatives or family members are around you, then you will be able to see them from time to time because your mind will accept this reality.

They also said that one day we would be able to see the other side through the use of a black light and green laser light frequency combination.

My Death Experience and the Other Side

I suffered a massive heart attack in January of 1997, and I had a quadruple bypass in January of 1998. During these events I died for a short while and was transported to the other side, here I met Jesus and two saints. They were floating above a cloud and I was floating towards them. Below I could see the Earth.

There are no words that can describe the happiness that I felt. I did not want to come back to Earth, I wanted to stay there. Unfortunately they pointed back down to Earth and told me that I had to go back and take care of unfinished business.

They showed me the United States and the disaster that is going to happen to Earth in the near future. I saw that a portion of California had separated from the border of Arizona and Nevada, the Sea of Cortez had expanded towards the top of Nevada and many great cities were gone and numerous people were dead and missing and gone forever. I'm not sure of the time line but it is possible that this will occur in the year 2010 or 2011. There will be a massive earth quake in California, registering 16.5 on the Richter scale.

Many of you do not believe this will ever happen in your lifetime, but it will happen sooner or later. There will be great geographical changes very soon.

The Angels told me that when the United State Government started exploding nuclear bombs and hydrogen bombs underground in the Nevada Desert, they caused the fault lines to start separating. This caused a domino effect of earth quakes in the past and continuing to occur in the future.

Other Information from the Angel Spirits

This information was given to me at different times throughout the day or different days of the week just out of the blue.

The Angels told me that we can avoid numerous disasters by getting at least one million people to join hands and pray. This prayer must concentrate on preventing or stopping whatever needs to be changed at the time.

But everyone must believe and be sincere for it to work.

The Angels told me drug addicts are usually people or individuals whose sub-consciously craves the euphoric feeling they once felt when they were on the other side.

Their souls have not learned how to readjust to this world. If you have ever had an afterlife experience then you can relate to this statement from the Angels.

They told me that, contrary to Christian teaching, there is reincarnation. We lived several lives based on what we learned in each life. For example:

If in one life you were able to comprehend the most important things in life and you were giving and unselfish, and you made efforts to help the sick and comfort people in their time of need and did whatever was in your capabilities at the time, you probably would not have to come back for a second time.

You keep coming back until you learn certain lessons in life that humble you and make you thankful for all the things that most people take for granted. Once you learn all the lessons in life then you no longer have to come back.

On the other hand if you are a jealous person, a greedy person, or a selfish person only thinking about yourself or if you speak ill will of others, then you shall keep on returning over and over in different economic levels and colors until you learn the important things in life.

They said that we are not supposed to know about reincarnation because some people will then continue to do bad things knowing they will get repeated chances to make things right...

Some psychics will have you believe that there are no punishments for your actions on earth, but in fact, there are severe punishments for those who commit horrendous crimes of murder and mayhem.

The Angels said that we should put Scientist in Political Offices, not Political Scientist in office, because for those who don't know the difference a

Politician is one who is trained in Political Science or the Art of Bull shitting the Public, the other is a Scientist who knows all about physics and chemistry and the effects of pollution on the earth.

On the Other Side

When you pass on, your relatives come to greet you and to explain everything that you will be going through.

For example, you will have to hang around on earth for forty days and forty nights, before you can journey on to heaven. During those forty days and nights you will be able to visit your relatives in their homes and hear all that they are saying about you, what type of person you were the good and bad things that you did.

When you finally go to the other side, you will find that men and women are separated from each other. The women relatives are all in one group, the men relatives are in another group. You can visit each other, but you not allowed staying together in case you get reassigned back to earth. In the beginning you have to attend reorientation classes explaining all the dos and don'ts, because you have rules everywhere you go.

You can create whatever life style you want on the other side and in any time period that you were used to living in.

When I have had contact with my relatives, I found out that this is the way it is on the other side.

You see there is no grief, no loneliness; no negative feeling of any kind. All you feel is indescribable love and forgiveness for everyone who has ever done you wrong.

You always have something to do over there and, you're never lonely. You are allowed to view your family or relatives from the other side and try to contact them through dreams or by sending animals or flowers that those persons can associate with you. I have known people who received some type of bird, flower, or butterflies, which hung around their home.

You learn about different things that people can do in the spirit world, how they can a-port you objects that have been lost to you and you get them back.

I have been blessed with these experiences throughout my life. I have lost several objects that have miraculous return to me out of nowhere. I have had other experiences from the other side and where things were explained to me.

For example spirits are capable of are making electronic objects work in different manners than usual, they can make a phone ring and the caller ID will show a phone number from a dead relative who number is no longer in use. They can make televisions and radios turn on and off.

Those are examples where they are trying to get your attention and they want you to make contact with them thru a psychic. So make the effort if the opportunity comes your way. There are a lot of good psychics out there, who are not phonies, stay away from gypsies and other whom require large sums of money to make contact for you.

Go to psychic fairs or new age stores in your area. That is where you are likely to meet reputable psychics who, and will usually charge approximately forty dollars, for half an hour, or eighty dollars, for a full hour.

An Angel took me into space in my astral form and showed me, a line of new souls waiting to be born. They were linked together, and glowed different shades of green in different patterns.

The Angels said that most humans are born with great mental capabilities, but that a genetic mental block is placed on us by God, because we were still to savage, and too war oriented to wield such mental powers. We have to be free of envy, jealous, greed, lust. That is why only being who ascend is capable of using 100% of their intellect, because they are free of all the bad human emotions.

Further, man has a history of destroying things it cannot comprehend, or control, or else it uses information and technology for war purposes.

How can we be contacted as a group of earthling if we are still too primitive and untrusting, and if our governments want to dissect every being they come in contact with or steal its technology for war purposes? We are a long way from contact with other being.

Genetic Memory

One fine example of genetic memory finger prints. If you cut a small piece of your finger tip, it will grow back, along with the original pattern of your finger prints.

Another example is facial features that you inherit from your parents. There is also mental genetic memory, which involves instincts. For example when we are born, a baby has the instinct to suckle on its mother's breast for feeding.

The Angels also explained that we also carry genetic memories from our ancestors: we sometimes inherit their past experiences.

There is a difference between our own past life experiences and genetic memory experiences inherited from our ancestors. I would have to go into more detail to try to explain to you how to tell the difference.

Another example of genetic physical change occurs when are minds are heightened with intellect and the awareness of other energies and the presence of higher beings.

A fine example of physical change is the case of Terry Schiavo, and others like her. If you look at Ms. Schiavo prior to her accident, her physical appearance is that of a normal individual. But after her accident, her physical appearance changes dramatically, because the brain has been injured. Once the brain has been injured, physical changes occur.

This is what happened to early man, as he grew smarter, his physical appearances started to change and evolve into a higher form of a new species of man.

Of course there were influences from the higher realm of God, which gave early man his awareness, which caused his physical attributes to gradually evolve.

Mankind progress is based on intellect and awareness of our physical universe and other forms of energy that are all around us, but we do not physically see.

Each generation slowly evolves into the next, higher human mind.

The Secret

For those of you, who have read The Secret or bought the video, I want you to know how these things relate to yourself and the Universe and your physical world.

The Angel said there are some truths to the Secret, such as willing something to happen, especially when you are young. The young are more magical because they are innocent and naïve, they don't limit themselves to what they believe. But it is possible for anyone to will something to happen.

For example if you want to grow taller, all you have to do is tell your body that you want to be taller and your mind will connect with your physical body and start to making you grow taller.

Another example is that of Soleil Moon Frye, who played Punky Brewster. She always wished that she had big boobs when she was a kid, and after wishing or willing it to be so, it actually happened to her, she grew tremendous boobs, but because she forgot to tell her body when she was satisfied with her size, she had to get breast reduction surgery later in her life.

Some young people have more will power than others and are able to make physical things happen, to themselves. Other young individuals lack will power or have low self esteems so they never evolve their physical bodies or personalities.

There are many factors involved such as different social back grounds and highly dysfunctional families...

Just remember what is normal to some people may not be normal to others. Different cultures may have practices or lifestyles that are consider taboo by some but may be the norm for others. If these people are not hurting anyone physically or mentally, then they should be allowed to practice their ways of life.

A fine example is nudist families. This is a very acceptable practice and should never be frowned upon as long as it is practiced, in a comfortable setting for all involved, and does not infringe on others personal space.

The Secret, will work for some and not for others. It is said that when are to be born, we write a life script how we want our life to be.

That is why each person has a different life, some of us are born poor, and we later become rich, or some of us struggle all our lives and never get ahead.

Other individuals seem to walk on water, everything just falls into place for them, and they get all the opportunities in the world. Some are meant for greatness either as a scientist, philosophers, actors, singers, and so on in different categories.

Some of us are just here to learn lessons about ourselves and life itself; therefore we come in different economic levels of life, because we have not yet learned what we are supposed to.

That is also why some people die at an early age, because they have fulfilled their goal ahead of time, and return to heaven. Some of us are here to mentor others and help them in this physical world to learn not only academically but also spiritually.

When we are born we have a set pattern for where we are going, and sometimes we have multiple choices for which direction to go in. But because we are affected by people who have bad intentions or are jealous we do not fulfill our intended journey.

So remember there are some truths to the Secret, depending on your age and beliefs.

God and Moses and Magical Seals

God gave Moses the knowledge of making seals that would make the Angels help him remove any obstacles and which also removed evil spirits or entities that possessed men, this knowledge was also given to the Kings of Israel, such as king Solomon and King David, this information was later given only to Kabala rabbis. Contrary to what some psychics will tell you, there are demons that roam the earth from time to time in different forms, and there is such a thing as possession by evil spirits.

That is why God gave Moses and others the magical seals to get rid of such entities. There is no higher magic or power than that of God and his Angels.

If you believe and pray every day and ask God and his Angels to come into your life and help guide you on your journey, they will be by your side, but you must always be sincere in your asking.

Angels and Saints

Another subject the Angels wanted me to bring up was the fact that some religious groups believe that we should only pray to God and not to his Angels or saints.

First of all God may be all seeing and knowing, but think about all the people in the world, he cannot hear every individual persons thoughts. This is why he has millions of Angels and spirit guides assigned to each of us.

The way it was explained to me was that in the beginning God spoke to Moses and told him how to contact the Angels to help him remove whatever obstacles, was in his way. This is how the Seals of Moses came to be.

In the beginning only Jewish kings like King Solomon and King David were allowed the knowledge of the Angelic Seals and how to summon Angels and spirits.

This knowledge was later passed down to rabbis that practiced the Kabala, and it was kept secret. Only rabbis were allowed such knowledge.

The common person was not allowed to directly communicate with Angels or heavenly spirits, because he would be asking for too many favors that were selfish in nature.

This continued up until the time that Jesus became man and wandered the earth with his apostles.

Upon his existence and his teaching he anointed his apostles with the gift of giving blessing and healing the sick and removing evil spirits and affliction from people...

This knowledge was passed down from one apostle to the next, so long as he was sincere and pious. Other individuals became favored as saints by God himself, because they were martyrs and were willing to die for their beliefs in Jesus and they gave up any selfish desires.

Because only Kabala rabbis were allowed Angel contact, they were unwilling to petition Angels to do special favors for common individuals.

So Jesus, changed things by appointing saints to represent the common man, these saints had once been human, so they were more understanding when it came to the needs of men and their cries for mercy.

In some instances, regular humans are allowed to make contact with Angels, because we believe and we care and we are humble. So we can teach others, or give messages or others from the other side.

Today, the Kabala teaching is readily available with research capabilities on the internet.'

The Kabala was meant for all mankind for learning wisdom, not for abusing Angelic energies. You see Angel magic is not to be used for doing bad deeds, because such action will come back on you three fold.

Many people do not understand this, which is why most Kabalist spend years meditations and prayers .regarding the uses and practices of the Kabala.

The Kabala is meant to teach wisdom and understanding of all that surrounds us.

It is very in depth, and most intellects will crave more knowledge and will want to read more about its history and practices, and about all the different books that relate to one another.

Nephilians

Another mention in the Bible are the nephilians, they were actually offspring of Angelic being that mated with humans. Some may still exist today, but most were hunted down and killed by other Angels of God, because God did not want humans with such powers to be roaming the earth. Man is still to barbaric and war mongering.

Some may have managed to live or showed that they were worthy so they were sterilized in order to prevent further offspring, and were allowed to live on the earth for hundreds of years.

Spirit Guides or Guardian Angels

What we call our guardian Angel is actually our spirit guide. Only people who were once alive and fulfilled their lessons are allowed to be spirit guides. The reason for this is that only someone who was once human, who shared all the emotions that you feel is capable of helping you. Angels have never been human so they cannot feel human emotion which leaves them unqualified to help you in human emotional decisions.

Angels help us in their own way. They are appointed by God to watch over the spirit guides and our future lessons which we go through with the help of our guides.

There are books and references on the internet which explain methods of making contact with your spirit guide.

Spirits and Ghosts

Spirits and ghosts are different. A Spirit is someone who is on the other side or heaven. A ghost is earthbound soul that cannot ascend into heaven for different reasons. Most ghosts are individuals who cannot accept their deaths, and refuse to go, such as sex maniacs, alcoholics, and gamblers and people with other vices.

In some cases the individual was murdered and refuses to ascend to heaven until his or her killer is brought to justice. Then that person can accept his or her death and ascend.

For example, some ghosts are murder victims whose bodies have not been recovered and given the proper funeral services. Individuals cannot ascend because their bodies have not had their remains brought to rest on holy ground.

Sign Language

Another thing the Angels told me was that if everyone was taught American Sign Language there would be no language barriers and communication with anyone would be easy. In the future sign language will be turned into a glyphic language that everyone will be able to read.

Man and the Earth

The Angels said that when man was put on this Earth, he was suppose to live in harmony, with nature and, but as man became more advanced, he created pollutions.

Now man is harming the planet.

They explained that the earth is a large living entity, much like us. Its rivers and lakes and oceans, are like our blood, and all the creatures that live on earth, are like the organisms which live in our bodies. We don't notice them, yet they live inside us helping us function every day.

When we pollute the earth we act like a cancer on the body, so the earth must fight to remove, the tumors that are affecting its health.

Natural disasters occur to cleanse the earth of too many people and the pollution in one area. It is the only way the earth has to cleanse and heal itself.

The Angels said that when we build tall buildings in one area, we create a great deal of geometric pressure in a small area, where water tables have been depleted. Therefore it is like a water bed metaphor.

As long as the water bed is full of water it will support the tremendous weight above. As the water table is depleted, and more weight is placed on the upper crust of the earth, then the crust will eventually give way to the massive weight being imposed on one small area.

If we continue to drain the water tables for fresh water usage and for irrigation purposes then we will start to have more subsidence and earthquakes.

Hurricanes and Tornados

The Angels said that in areas where there is tornado activity, we should build dome shaped, or wedge shape homes because they will not be affected by the whirling winds of a tornado.

In hurricane areas, we should also build dome shape homes or wedge shaped homes that can withstand high winds. The wind would ramp over the top of homes without causing any damage.

They explained to me different ways of accomplishing these designs on pre-existing homes.

They Angels said that levies are inadequately built; they should have triangular wing walls coming off the wall every one hundred feet.

They told me that we could stop hurricanes by exploding five-hundred pound concussion bombs in a triangular pattern near the eye of the hurricane, between the height of hurricane and the ocean surface. They said we could also drop blocks of Ice from cargo planes, this would dissipate the whirling affect.

The Homeless

They told me how we could help the homeless find jobs and receive benefits that are entitled to them.

They said the biggest problem for homeless people is that they don't have an address to receive benefits and to apply for a job and they don't have phone number, or message center to receive messages for job calls.

They said that with all the city or municipal parks, the existing park building could be used to give the homeless post office boxes that several families could use share.

Them those entitled to benefits such as unemployment and healthcare could receive them...

The park buildings would give these people a place for job interviews and showering as well as a place a place to receive phone calls or messages for jobs.

These centers could also provide clothes donated by communities to the homeless and their families.

This would also create jobs at the Park centers, for example, there would have to be mail handlers to sort the mail for these P.O. Boxes and dispatch the forgoing mail to the proper recipients or families and deliver the forgoing mail to the proper recipients or families assigned to these post office boxes.

The Angels gave me more specific details on how to make everything work, but that would require much more time to go into the details.

Quantum Soul

Another subject explained to me was quantum soul experiences. This has to do with our souls being quantum, which means we exist in the past and in the present and in the future.

The Angels said we actually live in the past, even though we think we live in the present.

The future exists far ahead of us and we are just following a life pattern that is already set for us.

Because we existed in the past, present and future we were able to see backwards and forward in time. Our souls are connected to each other in all time periods, which is why some people are able to glance into the future.

We also exist in alternate dimensions or alternate worlds. There are a total of seventy two dimensions of earth.

To our misfortune, we are tied to some of our other selves in those alternate worlds. That is why we sometimes feel a great sadness, or we start crying for no reason at all. In those instances, our other self is experiencing grief, or some type of tragedy. Since some of us are more connected than others we feel the emotions.

We have many reasons for our various displays of emotions, some of us are connected to other people in our lives and we feel when they are in danger and or in some type of trouble.

Déjà vu and Reincarnation

There are many situations of déjà vu, where we dream an event or situation and then at some future point find yourselves actually living the event exactly as you dream it.

A variation of this has to do with re-incarnation.

Have you ever met someone for the first time, but for some reason, you felt great resentment toward that person. Some of you will understand what I'm saying.

Or perhaps just the opposite happened; you meet someone for the first time and felt that you knew them, even though you have never met.

I have found myself in both those situations, and I have been to places and yet I recognize the locations and building as though I had been there before.

I have had many beautiful experiences, thanks to the Angels, my spirit guides and their wisdom.

Other Abilities and Experiences

Something that most people don't know about me is that when I close my eyes, I don't see darkness. I see bright colors; it is like having the lights on all the time.

Sometimes I see the truth regarding the paternity of a child. I see the image of the true father come out of the child, and it is not the man assumed to be the father.

I do not disclose the truth in those situations because the one who suffers is the child. The child need not know the truth, unless it is a matter of life and death, such as a kidney transplant or special blood transfusion.

I can also look into a person's eyes and know if they have murdered someone. It's an eerie feeling.

If you want to know what it is like being me, rent the movies; The Gift with Cate Blanchet, and

Katie Holmes, and Eyes of Laura Mars with Faye Dunaway.

It is not easy having these gifts, and being empowered with vast knowledge and experiences.

It becomes very frustrating not being able to tell someone about the information being given to me.

I constantly hear voices of the departed whispering in my ears and at night they yell. They constantly were trying to get my attention. They throw objects around, they move small objects.

I learned how to turn them off with a prayer given to me by another psychic.

Lord Heavenly Father, please surround me with your Divine White Light and the Golden Light of the Holy Spirit and protect me from all evil seen and unseen. Let your most holy Angels dwell here among us to protect us and watch over us and to protect us from all evil seen and unseen.

This prayer always works, but I don't know how to turn on my powers afterwards, so I have to wait to receive messages.

The Sun is a Black Hole

Another thing told to me by the Angels was that our sun is actually a black hole. It is burning gases from space but when it runs out the hole will form and inverted space energy will start to take place.

How to Harm Beings from the Fourth Dimension

The Angels also told me to tell you that creatures from the fourth dimension cannot be harmed by lead, brass, or copper bullets. That is why bullets have no affect when people have encountered Bigfoot.

These creatures can only be harmed by iron or silver bullets, which you cannot purchase at any sporting goods store. Therefore, you will not have any effect on creatures from the fourth dimension.

The Bible Code

You know I find it interesting that the Bible code people are never able to predict events until after they have happened.

If the Bible code really worked then, the people who believe in it would know future events before anyone else.

You have to remember that the Bible has been rewritten over and over again from its original version, so in reality the Bible code is nonsense.

Having Alternate Experiences from Blood Transfusions or Transplants

I have heard that some individuals who received organ transplants often experience personality changes.

I experienced them after receiving six pints of blood from my open heart surgery. For example, I did not like sports before the surgery, but afterwards I became a sports nut for a while. There were certain foods that I did not like to eat, but after the transfusion, I started craving different foods that I previously did not care for.

I believe that I experienced different behavioral attitudes that I did not have before, as well as some of the life experiences of the people from whom I received blood.

I experienced alternate life realities, which seemed so real, but in fact they were not. It was good that I was able to distinguish between what was real and what was not.

Some of you who have had transplants or blood transfusions may share similar experiences.

What I Was Told Regarding UFO's and Aliens

This is going to get in depth about certain realities, that surround us, and some people cannot accept the truth or find it hard to believe what I was told by the Angels.

Long before our generation of man existed, there were different beings living on Earth. They are still living here today, only in a different frequency of this dimension.

You see, numerous alien structures are all around us, on earth and numerous space ships come and go from other galaxies. We happen to see them from time to time as they enter our atmosphere, and then they have to set their space craft to the right frequency for their dimension where they exist.

To try to understand this, look at a radio. Between the dial of 1014 and 1015 there may be ten different frequencies. This is the same principal in our third dimension there are different frequencies, before reaching the 4th dimension. In one of these frequencies is where our alien friends are living side by side with us. They have our best interest at heart, which is why they have destroyed certain missiles that we launched in years past, especially any type of nuclear weapons that posed a threat to their frequency dimension as well as ours.

When we deploy these types of weapons we create rifts in the fields of time and dimension... Many of these rifts continue for extended time periods and appear and disappear throughout time.

This is how the Bermuda Triangle and other similar locations were formed. Some rifts occurred before our time due to meteor activity and other cosmic collusions.

Some of these, phenomena, are due in part to ancient alien technology which is still active in some parts of the world under this dimension.

The true reality is that a lot of energies and infrastructures are hidden from us by cloaking through the alternate frequency dimension.

From time to time, I have been able to time to view some beings and planets that are very close to the earth and yet no one else can see them because they are cloaked under some type of energy.

There are many beings and structures hidden from the average person's eyes. Most people are not allowed to know the truth to prevent mass panic. People cannot handle the truth.

I was told that some aliens are actually us in the future and that they come back in time to capture the DNA from this time period in order to regain some of their humanity, and certain abductees actually hold the special DNA strands that they seek.

The Angels said this happened when they were experimenting with reptilian DNA and insect DNA, to help them, survive viruses and diseases in the near future, but in the process they lost their human looking physical qualities.

The Dark Ages

The Angels explained to me talk of demons or monsters, and wizards and sorcerers, in the Dark Ages.

Some beings or creatures were named by ignorant humans. The groups were actually ancient races of beings that were stranded here and persecuted by man because they looked different from us.

Those poor beings were killed just because of their looks, which is how hate grew between our races. Man has always tried to kill that which does not look or appear like him, and that which he cannot understand or control.

Ancient Technology

Sorcerers and wizards were actually humans from the future who had advance technology. Because ancient man was so ignorant and did not know what technology was, they taught it was some type of magic.

For those of you who follow documentaries on inventors and advanced technology, you will know that an individual is able to focus energy on certain objects and make them levitate. This was demonstrated by an inventor named John Hutchison, and others like him were also shown on a show which use to come out on G4 channel called Invent This. The Federal Government later confiscated the inventor's equipment and kept the technology for them. This is similar to the ancient's technology that was used to levitate giant stones into place in the mountains of Peru, in Machu Picchu.

If you notice, it was the minority races who were the most advanced in architectural structures and building, hundreds of years more advanced than other white races.

This falls back into the spiritual realm; these people were tied to the spiritual realm and were receiving information on how to build and how to communicate with their ancestors.

Astral Projection

Through the use of meditation and herbs, the ancients were able to astral project into the sky and look down to see the shapes of lakes and land formations and islands. That is how they gave names to some objects that could only be seen from the skies

It is also how many Polynesians knew where islands and other land masses were, which showed them what direction to go.

Many Native Americans describe flying like an Eagle and views of the ground from above; when actually they did not realize that they were actually astral projecting from above the ground.

I too have been able to astral project and view land formation from above.

Failed Civilizations

Now the Angels want me to discuss why many ancient civilizations failed. If you look at the Aztecs and Mayan civilizations you can see simple things needed to keep such large groups of people going. They needed a great deal of food, which caused overhunting. Increased firewood usage let to deforestation which further depleted the environment. They also had to figure out what to do with all the feces, produced. There were no waste treatment facilities, which eventually led to diseases and plagues. The lesson was that in order to survive they had to spread out into the land.

Nicola Tesla

The Angels want me to talk about Mr. Nicola Tesla. This man and others like him was given to us by God to bring about change regarding our fossil fuel consumption and the pollution of the earth and its atmosphere.

Mr. Tesla was suppose to change lives, which he did, but he was also to show us how to quit using over polluting vehicles.

But since the oil industry controls everything, including members of Congress, pollution from vehicles is unlikely to change anytime soon, unless another country is willing to take the first step to create and export newer vehicles that run on hydrogen fuel or electricity.

Much technology has been suppressed by the oil industry and by members of Congress so that we will always be dependent on the oil Industry, for our fuels.

The oil industry and members of congress don't want you to know about the many geniuses that were killed after discovering alternate fuel sources.

It is a shame that we live in a world of greed, and selfishness, world where these corporation have killed innocent people just for profit.

Look up free energy websites on the internet and you will see some of the alternate energy sources available.

You will find cars that were made to strictly run on Hydrogen fuel, in which the hydrogen was being processed as the car was in motion.

You can find out about magnetic generators that produce great amounts of electricity, without any use of gasoline or a battery.

There are a lot of geniuses, whom have learned to harness these alternate energies, but unfortunately some have been killed and you know by whom.

Look up free energy websites on the internet and you will see some of the alternate energy sources available. None of these magnetic generators would be possible, if not for the genius of Nicola Tesla; industry owes a lot to the genius of this man.

What I Was Told about Jesus

The Angels led me from Catholicism to Judaism, they told me the only true Bible is the Jewish bible, however contrary to Jewish belief, and Jesus is the Messiah.

God sent his son so when Judgment arrives, he God, will be able to judge man based on his son's human emotional experiences.

God cannot judge man if he does not know what it is to be human and have human emotions and endure temptations.

You see God and his Angels cannot feel human emotions except for Love, but Jesus experienced humanity. Therefore, the Father was able to experience human emotion through his son, which makes him able to pass judgments on mankind when the time comes.

The Angels told me that the Bible is only a guide for how to live one's life, should not be taken word for word as the truth.

They said to remember man wrote the Bible not God and many parts of the Bible were greatly exaggerated. The Bible was written three hundred years after the actual events took place.

Jesus' job was to bring all men together Gentiles and Jews. Under the laws of Moses only circumcised Jews were allowed into Heaven, and then Jesus came to offer entrance as long as people believed in him as the Savior.

Remember, Jesus did not say I'm going to start Christian belief. He was a devoted Jew and under no circumstances would he change his religion. His only purpose was to unite all the people together as one.

His real name was Yoshoua Barrasabas. The name Jesus Christ was given to him by Emperor Constantine.

The Jewish Bible called Jesus by his true first name, because all these characters in the Bible had Hebrew names.

The Angels said contrary to the Bible we are not supposed to return to Israel. This supposed inspiration was a false promise given by the Devil to bring the downfall of man.

If the Jewish people try to fulfill the promise of returning to Israel, it will bring Armageddon. Why would anybody want to bring the end of the world by following a false promise?

The Angels said that when the appropriate time comes for all men to perish and be judged, there is no reason for Armageddon type war or destruction. It will not matter where in the world you are located; you will perish and be judged.

The Angels said men have committed great atrocities towards each other in the name of God, by bearing false witness against other men, and by taking it upon themselves to be the judges of other men.

The great witch hunts that certain churches practiced were all against the teachings of Jesus Christ.

He taught peace, tolerance, forgiveness, and acceptance of others, not burning people at the stake or torturing them for false prosecutions.

Jesus was here to break the old practices of the Jewish faith given to Moses by God. He was sent to change the practices for greater acceptance of others particularly uncircumcised Gentiles into the house of God...

He was not there to create a new religion, certainly not a religion that would include killing non believers in his name, and killing those, who would not conform to a made up religion.

The Angels said that the Bible was written with different interpretations, and by different religions that had their own agendas, or wanted to impose different beliefs on their particular religious groups.

What I found about Myself and My Origins

Well the Angels led me to the Web (www.sephardim. com), which gives the surnames of Sephardic Jews who left Israel and settled in Spain, France, Italy, and Germany.

Another Web site, the (History of the Sephardic Jews); describes the exodus and History of Jews in Spain.

I found out that I am actually of Sephardic Jewish descent, and that most families of Spanish, French, and Italian ancestry were actually Sephardic Jews, who lost their heritage due to the Crusades and the enforcement of Catholicism upon these countries by the Papal authorities.

So now I'm embracing my Jewish heritage, and religion. I found a Rabbi and other Jews who keep their faith but believe in Jesus as the Messiah, the Messianic Jews.

Remember Jesus was Jewish and he never changed his religion. Messianic Jews are the same as Jesus.

The Sephardic Jews are the true descendants of King David and King Solomon and the true members of the twelve tribes.

The vast majority of Hispanics are of Jewish ancestry. Our origins were erased due to the work of the Papal authorities. They passed laws forbidding the practices of Judaism, which is why Hispanics are not circumcised. The Papal laws forbade any such practices, and if you were found to be practicing Judaism, you were tortured, killed or burned at the stake for everyone to see.

To find out more of about the history of the Sephardic Jews, look up the Web sites mentioned above and the links that follow the web sites.

Photos of Angel Orbs Floating around Me

Above is a Polaroid picture of me taken for my job and the angelic orbs appeared? You can see them going in and out of my body in different locations. They are always feeding me information. I am constantly receiving messages and images of different people and events.

This is the real deal; if you look closely you can see them inside my body at different positions. I don't know why I was chosen to receive messages. I often wonder why someone in a higher position doesn't receive these messages, and the Angels told me people in higher offices don't believe in spirits or Angels. Their faith is lacking, and that is why they are not chosen to receive messages.

Spirit Realms

As I mentioned there is a difference between spirits and ghosts and their dimensions or planes or realms or levels.

There are different levels of spirit realms due to religious beliefs. This is because God is merciful towards us, so he has created different locations for different circumstances.

I hope that I can explain this to the best of the knowledge given to me by the Angels.

It was explained to me that Christians and whoever else accepted Jesus as the Messiah, would go to the highest realm in heaven.

There are exceptions; the early followers of Moses, who followed all of Moses' teachings prior to the arrival of Jesus, would also go to the highest realms of Heaven.

But the people, who did not accept Jesus as the Messiah, would not be punished severely, as long as they believed in God the Father.

These worshippers would go to a different realm of Heaven, which varies slightly from the higher realm of Jesus' worshippers.

Some of may be wondering about the other religions such as Hindus, Buddhists,   and so on. These categories fall into the ghost realms, which I will explain in the next section you may better understand.

Ghost Realms

First of all let me once again explain that a ghost is someone who is earthbound and for different reasons was unable to go to Heaven.

I shall try to clarify as much as I can on the ghost realms and why they exist and how all this ties in with different cultures and religions and native or tribal people of the world.

As I said earlier, God is merciful towards people of other beliefs and those who are ignorant or lack knowledge of who he is. This is why there are different levels in the ghost realms for the earth- bound souls.

Let's start with the native or tribal people of the world, who have no concept of Christianity, this rule applies to native or tribal people of the world, they are not allowed into Heaven, but instead they exist in a ghost plane, which is very much like the world they lived in. Life there is peaceful and they are with relatives, and they gather food and hunt just like in real life, some don't even know they are dead.

This same rule applies to the other religions of the world that are non Christian, except for those who believe in Father God.

This applies to Hindus, Buddhist, and other religion that does not acknowledge Father God or the Messiah Jesus.

Now let's talk about the Islamic faith and their different situations. First of all let me say that the Angels said it was not for man to judge other men, this is only for God to do so upon the end of one's life, except in the case of civil laws concerning killing, stealing and other such laws.

Those who follow the laws of Islam and lead peaceful lives shall go to the second plane in heaven.

Those who kill and oppress people and commit suicide in order to kill others who do not share their beliefs shall not enter heaven. Instead, they shall go to some level of hell where they shall be severely punished for misrepresenting the will of Father God.

People must be given free will, to believe or not believe. Religion should not be forced on other men against their will. Only Father God can judge those who are non-believers.

Suicide

Let's talk about suicide. There are different circumstances involving suicide, some of which are acceptable in the eyes of heaven while others are not.

The Angels said that if you commit suicide in an act of valor, in order to save other people in a selfless act then, you shall be forgiven and allowed into heaven.

I you commit suicide because you are being tortured; this is another exception in which you will be forgiven and allowed into heaven.

If you commit suicide just to quit the life that you are in, this is unforgiveable and you will not be allowed into heaven. Instead you will go to a ghost realm.

If you commit suicide as a religious suicide bomber this is unforgivable and you will be sent to a plane of hell for having killed others beside yourself for acts that God does not accept.

Homosexuality

I wanted to know what the Angels had to say concerning this topic, and this is what they explained to me.

First of all, most forms of homosexuality have to do with reincarnation, except for a small percentage which has to do with other circumstances.

Throughout different lifetimes, if one was a man, then he kept choosing to come back as a man. This also applies to being a woman and to continue to come back as a woman.

In some instances, a woman decides that she wants to come back as a man, but upon being born she forgets that she chose a man's body and feels out of place knowing deep down inside that she is a woman and not a man.

This also occurs with a man wanting to come back as a woman rather than a man. Upon being born, she starts to have orientation problems with the gender that has been chosen.

The problem with reincarnation is that we don't remember making those choices once we are reborn into a new life. It is very hard for some individuals to accept their new choice, knowing deep inside that they are the opposite gender.

The Angels said that once these individuals made choices, they should learn to live with their choices until their deaths, and make the most of their situation.

The Angel said if they choose to practice homosexuality, then they should do so in quietly in the homes and should not flaunt their sexuality in the open.

The Angels understand that all humans need love and understanding in their lives, and yes, they made a mistake in picking the gender that they wanted to be born in, but they must make the most of it, one way or another.

There are other individuals who did not choose opposite gender reincarnation roles, but instead were molested and aroused by someone of the same sex. This caused them much confusion about their sexuality.

God understands this is no fault of their own and only asks that they keep their sexuality practices discreet, so as not to entice others into the same practices.

Imprint Energy

Imprint energy is energy that is left behind and keeps repeating itself following some traumatic incident. This could include a murder or some other violent act, even arguments with your spouse or loved ones.

You will see the event play over. The event that took place and the individuals who caused this to happen will appear as transparent figures or ghosts but in actuality they are not; their energy is caught in time and continues to repeat itself as an anomaly.

There are ways to rid the location of the imprint energy through cleansing rituals provided by those who practice the spiritual arts and know what they are doing with herbs and spells.

Abortion

I wanted to know what the Angels had to say on the subject matter of abortion. This is what I was told. They said since we had free will, it was up to the individual to make this decision. Abortion was forgivable, depending on the circumstances and it was not up to other people to judge an individual for having an abortion. Only God will judge that person when her time comes up.

They said that an actual soul does not enter the body until approximately three months to six months of the gestation period of pregnancy depending on the reincarnated soul's decision to enter the body.

Yes from the fetus to approximately six months of gestation it is alive in a biological manner but not in the sense of the soul having entered the body, it functions are simply reflex.

For women who were victims of rape, abortion is acceptable. For women who had hardships or whose life would be endangered due to a pregnancy this is also acceptable.

Women who aborted children just to abort them time after time and who did not practice birth control would be judged by God.

The Angels said that all the anti-abortion groups should be going out and adopting these unwanted kids who are in orphanages or foster homes, which are looking to be adopted by some body, if they are so adamant about abortion.

The Angels asked if people who oppose abortion are going to support these unwanted children. Are the church's going to financially support these unwanted children?

The Angels said that most people are quick to judge others but don't give themselves a good look. What are they doing for all those unwanted children that someone gave up for adoption? The ones who are still out there waiting to be adopted? If they really care about these future unborn children, then they should be adopting as many foster children as they can afford.